Simple Machines in Compound Machines

by Oliver Garcia

PEARSON

Scott
Foresman

Editorial Offices: Glenview, Illinois • Parsippany, New Jersey • New York, New York
Sales Offices: Needham, Massachusetts • Duluth, Georgia • Glenview, Illinois
Coppell, Texas • Ontario, California • Mesa, Arizona

Photographs

Every effort has been made to secure permission and provide appropriate credit for photographic material. The publisher deeply regrets any omission and pledges to correct errors called to its attention in subsequent editions.

Unless otherwise acknowledged, all photographs are the property of Pearson Education, Inc.

Photo locators denoted as follows: Top (T), Center (C), Bottom (B), Left (L), Right (R), Background (Bkgd)

Cover (R) ©Royalty-Free/Corbis, (T) Nomad_Soul/Fotolia; **3** (TR) ©Royalty-Free/Corbis, (B) ©Siede Preis/Getty Images; **5** Nomad_Soul/Fotolia; **7** Faraways/Shutterstock; **9** (BR) ©Royalty-Free/Corbis; **10** (BL) ©Royalty-Free/Corbis; **11** (BR, BL, BC) ©Royalty-Free/Corbis, (B) ©Siede Preis/Getty Images; **12** ©Royalty-Free/Corbis; **13** Anyaivanova/Fotolia; **14** (BC) ©Royalty-Free/Corbis, (BL) Getty Images.

ISBN: 0-328-13225-X

Look at the things in the picture. Do you know how they are all alike? They are all machines. A machine is anything that makes work easier.

Some of the machines in the picture are very simple. They work with just one movement. They are called **simple machines**.

Some of the machines are not so simple. They are made of two or more simple machines. They are called **compound machines**.

Simple Machines

We use simple machines and compound machines every day. Let's start with simple machines. There are six simple machines. Take a look at the picture. It shows you what they are.

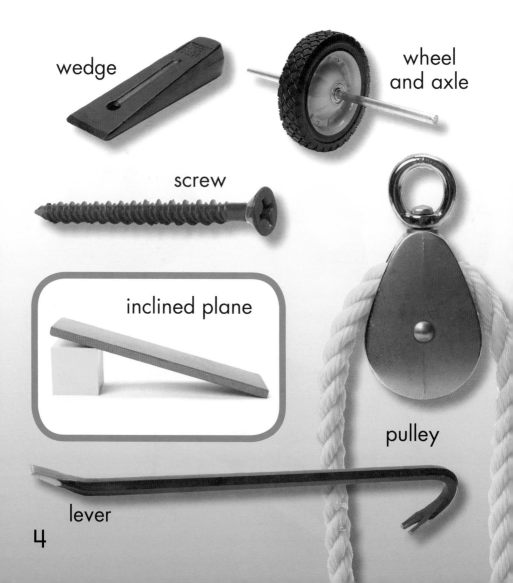

wedge

wheel and axle

screw

inclined plane

pulley

lever

Wheel and Axle

If you have seen a bike or a car roll down the street, then you have seen a wheel and axle in action.

The wheel and axle is a simple machine. The axle is a kind of rod, or bar, that goes through the wheel. The wheel and axle turn together and help things move.

Bikes, Ferris wheels, wagons, and cars all use wheels and axles to move.

Lever

Have you ever been on a seesaw? When you sit on one end, the person on the other end goes up in the air.

A seesaw is a type of lever. The lever is a very simple machine. If you push down on one end, the other end goes up. A lever can be great for lifting things.

You can also pull a lever up. When you do that, the other end goes down. That is a useful thing, too. Think of a wheelbarrow. Its handles are levers. When you lift them up, the wheelbarrow tilts down. Then you can roll the wheelbarrow.

Other levers include a shovel, a bottle opener, and a nutcracker.

What will happen if the girl pushes down on her side of the lever?

Pulley

A pulley is another kind of simple machine used for lifting things. There are two parts to a pulley. A pulley uses a special kind of wheel. It also has something that goes around the wheel, such as a chain or a rope.

When you pull on one end of the rope or chain, whatever is attached to the other end goes up. Cranes are a kind of pulley.

Inclined Plane

In one picture below, a boy is lifting a heavy box. In the other picture, a boy is using a ramp. Which do you think is easier to do?

It is easier to use a ramp. That is because it takes a lot less **force**, or energy, to push the box up a ramp than to lift it up.

A ramp is an inclined plane. An inclined plane has a flat surface, like a board. It is higher at one end than the other.

You use inclined planes to move things up or down. A ramp, a slanted road, a path up a hill, and a playground slide are all inclined planes.

Wedge

Did you know that a knife is a machine? A knife uses a wedge to cut things. A wedge is another simple machine.

A wedge is two inclined planes joined back-to-back. It uses force to go between two things.

The head of an ax is also a wedge. It goes between the wood and splits it apart.

The last simple machine is the screw. We use screws for joining things together. Legs are screwed to a table. Bookshelves can be screwed into walls.

Screws use an inclined plane wrapped around a small pole or tube. The inclined plane on a screw is called a thread. Threads make it easier for a screw to go up or down.

A lid on a jar of jelly is a kind of screw. When you want to close the jar, you turn the lid in a circle. Because the lid is a screw, it moves down onto the jar and closes it tightly.

thread

10

Compound Machines

Now that you know what simple machines are, you are ready to learn about compound machines. You may remember that a compound machine is made up of two or more simple machines working together.

Look at the scissors in the picture. Can you figure out which three simple machines are in that pair of scissors?

lever

axle

wedge

A pair of scissors uses levers. When you push down on the top handle of a pair of scissors, the bottom blade comes up.

A pair of scissors also uses wedges. The blades of the scissors are shaped like wedges. The blades cut through a material just like an ax cuts through wood.

A pair of scissors also uses a screw as an axle that holds the scissors together.

The three simple machines in a pair of scissors really help to make it a useful **gadget**.

Another **convenient** piece of **equipment** is a wheelbarrow. A wheelbarrow is a compound machine. It has two simple machines in it.

As you read earlier, the handles of the wheelbarrow are levers. If you pull up on them, the wheelbarrow tilts down.

Can you figure out what the other simple machine in a wheelbarrow is? It is a wheel and axle.

There are lots of other compound machines. See how many you can find around your house or school.

levers

Now Try This

There are many different kinds of compound machines that make our lives easier and more fun.

Bikes, buses, fans, staplers, toys, and even can openers are all compound machines. They help us push, open, or lift things. They help people and things get from one place to another. They make our lives better.

All machines were invented by someone. Now it is your turn. Invent a compound machine that will help you do something. Use some of the simple machines that you read about in this book.

Here's How To Do It!

Follow these five steps to create your own compound machine.

1. Think about what you want your machine to do.

2. Think about which simple machines can help.

3. Draw a picture of your machine. Label the parts.

4. Write about your machine. Write two to three sentences explaining what it can do.

5. Name your machine!

Glossary

compound machines *n.* machines that are made out of two or more simple machines working together.

convenient *adj.* helpful (used to describe a thing, not a person).

equipment *n.* supplies.

force *n.* a push, pull, or twist that makes something move.

gadget *n.* a small device or machine.

simple machines *n.* machines that do work with just one movement.